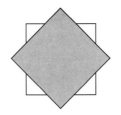

Quilts by
Paul D. Pilgrim

Blending the Old & the New

Gerald E. Roy

Located in Paducah, Kentucky, the American Quilter's Society (AQS), is dedicated to promoting the accomplishments of today's quilters. Through its publications and events, AQS strives to honor today's quiltmakers and their work – and inspire future creativity and innovation in quiltmaking.

EXECUTIVE EDITOR:	JANE R. MCCAULEY
CONTRIBUTING EDITOR:	VICTORIA FAORO
BOOK & ILLUSTRATIONS DESIGN:	ANGELA SCHADE
COVER:	KAREN CHILES
PHOTOGRAPHY:	CHARLES R. LYNCH, UNLESS OTHERWISE NOTED

Library of Congress Cataloging-in-Publication Data

Roy, Gerald E.
    Quilts by Paul D. Pilgrim: blending the old & the new / Gerald E. Roy.
       p. 80 cm.
    ISBN 0-89145-848-4
    1. Patchwork. 2. Patchwork. 3. Quilts.
  I. Title.
    TT779.M37 1995   94-38946
    746.46–dc20   CIP

Additional copies of this book may be ordered from: American Quilter's Society, P.O. Box 3290, Paducah, KY 42002-3290 @ $16.95. Add $2.00 for postage & handling.

Printed in the U.S.A. by Image Graphics, Paducah, KY

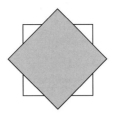

Dedication

In memory of Irene and Ray Pilgrim, who encouraged their son to dream.

In achieving his dreams, he more than fulfilled theirs — and touched many along the way.

Thank you for your gift.

Acknowledgments

There are many people to thank for helping make possible exhibits of Paul's work and this book.

Before the exhibit "Pilgrim's Progress: Paul D. Pilgrim, Blending the Old & the New" could be installed for the first time at the Museum of the American Quilter's Society in June 1996, many quilt tops had to be quilted and bound. We turned to family and friends for help. In preparation for the publication of this book and the installation of a memorial exhibit of Paul's quilts at the Museum of the American Quilter's Society in April 1997, I've again called on these people for help.

For their help and support, thanks go to:

- *My family, who loved Paul as a son and a brother*

- *Toni Fisher for putting everything aside and quilting so fast and furiously*

- *My sisters, Georgene Smith and Annette Kincaid; to my cousin, Corrine Pratt; and to friends, Bettina Havig, Sally Collins, and Helen Thompson for preparing the quilts for exhibition*

- *Glendora Hutson, without whose help I would never have been able to care for Paul full-time*

- *Vicki Faoro who, as always, has been a treasured friend to both of us*

- *All those who gave so much to Paul and me during his life and cared for me after Paul's death — a special thanks.*

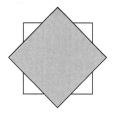

Contents

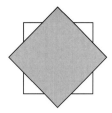

Preface

This book was written during Paul's last months, and this preface during the last few days I shared with him and in the week that followed his death. We were very fortunate to have had time to gather the information for his book together.

Though I had shared work space with Paul for many years, I had never really studied his quilts until I curated his June 1996 exhibit at the Museum of the American Quilter's Society: "Pilgrim's Progress: Quilts by Paul D. Pilgrim, Blending the Old and the New."

He always worked very privately on his quilts, making them very much "his own." He produced a number of quilts for reasons other than his own personal expression, but the quilts in this exhibit and this book are those I call "his own work." They were created solely to satisfy his own needs. They were not made for sale or even for show — just for him.

As he worked, Paul would ask "What do you think?" only after the top was completed. He neither welcomed suggestions, nor sought approval during the creative process. Friends and students can attest to the fact that this privacy was confined only to his work. Otherwise, his willingness to share his knowledge and expertise was boundless. His enthusiasm bordered on exhaustion for those less enthusiastic; it was only exceeded by his high energy and wonderful sense of humor.

I personally spent much time trying to keep up with him or at least stay out of the dust he kicked up as he sped along. His opinions were always forthcoming, sometimes outrageous, and would often lead to volatile discussions. He was a valuable member of any board. His generosity was not limited to the time he donated to a cause, but extended beyond. It also provided an outlet for his shopping addiction. The quilts we see today are the result of his shopping, buying, and collecting, in combination with his artistic taste and fine arts training.

Paul's depth of appreciation was shaped by the fact that he had an amazing range of skills. He was accomplished in many of the fine arts and crafts. He received his master's degree in jewelry design and fabrication and taught arts and crafts and art history on the junior high school level for ten years. He was a skilled designer and draftsman; many homes in the Bay Area reflect his talents. Quilters may be familiar with the Pilgrim/Roy fabric collections. His parents instilled in him the idea that he could do anything he put his mind to, and he believed it.

He learned to sew from an aunt on his mother's side who felt everyone should know at least how to put in a zipper — especially a man. However, it was from his father's side of the family that he inherited his quiltmaking interest. His grandmother, Sara Laura Shipman (Pilgrim) of Tennessee, was an experienced quiltmaker. After her death, Paul's grandfather remarried. At the time of his grandfather's death, his second wife disappeared, taking with her all the family belongings, including the quilts. It was not until Paul's parents retired and moved from Coalinga to Oakhurst that an unfinished wool quilt top and scraps were discovered in a blanket chest. Laura had started this quilt for Paul's father, using wool scraps from the children's clothing.

Paul finished this quilt and presented it to his father, Ray, on Christmas Day, 1978. It was a very emotional moment, for Ray recognized many fabrics from his childhood. Paul had begun making quilts in 1975, but it was this experience that caused him to start looking for old blocks, tops, and fabrics to incorporate in his quilts. For the rest of his life he continued shopping for just the right bits and pieces of the past.

It was not until I began studying his quilts for the exhibit selection that I began to discover what was so unique about the quilts Paul made using blocks and tops created in the past. These quilts are strong, clear, and confident statements — just as he was. Each quilt has a single purpose and clarity. Each one has a confidence and strength not compromised by ambiguity or ambition. His direct manner comes through in his work. His signature in fabric is as consistent as was his personality — and as direct!

When "Pilgrim's Progress" was first installed at the Museum of the American Quilter's Society, there were 16 quilts in the exhibit. Since that time 13 more quilts have been added, bringing the total to 29, all of which have become part of the museum's collection.

The last five quilts I discovered after Paul's death. They had been put away with backs he had prepared for sending out for quilting. He had forgotten about them and so had I. Unfortunately, I was not able to secure information about these from Paul, but Toni Fisher, who has quilted all of Paul's quilts, willingly agreed to quilt these as well; they are included in this book.

It gives me great comfort to know that Paul's work will be cared for and enjoyed by many people through exhibits and this publication. As we might have expected, Paul continues to give in death as he did so unselfishly in life.

GERALD E. ROY
NOVEMBER 1996

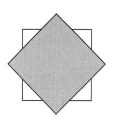

Paul D. Pilgrim
1942 – 1996

Artist

Teacher

Collector

Appraiser

Designer

Mentor

& Friend

On November 12, 1996, the quilt world lost a great talent and friend when Paul D. Pilgrim died of cancer at his home in Oakland, California. Born on November 9, 1942, in the small town of Coalinga, California, Paul was the only child of Ray and Irene Pilgrim.

The youngest of six children, Paul's mother, Irene La Hargue, was of French Basque and Spanish heritage. Her father had immigrated to this country, arriving in California just after the 1906 San Francisco earthquake. His first employment was clearing debris from the quake. He then traveled to Coalinga, opened a French laundry, and sent to Spain for his bride. He and the family owned and operated the laundry until he retired.

Paul's father, Lee Ray Pilgrim, was from a family tracing its roots to England, many generations earlier. Ray Pilgrim had a twin brother, Paul, and was one of eight children. His parents were ranchers and farmers in Porterville, California. Ray talked of being half Texan and half Oklahoman because the house he was born in straddled the border between the two states.

Ray and Irene were married just before Ray left to fight in World War II. Irene was just 17. Paul was born before Ray returned from the army. He had been injured in France and had received a Purple Heart. Paul was named not only for his father's twin brother, but also for General Eisenhower, whom Ray greatly admired and under whom he had served. Paul's middle name was Dwight.

Paul attended Coalinga public schools and junior college. He received a B.A. in education from California College of Arts and Crafts and an M.F.A. in jewelry design from Mills College, in Oakland. In 1969, he and his partner Gerald E. Roy founded Pilgrim/Roy Antiques and Interiors in Oakland.

A man of many talents, Paul will be remembered as a nationally recognized artist, teacher, designer, collector, quiltmaker, quilt judge, and certified quilt appraiser. Together with Gerald E. Roy, he helped to establish and develop the AQS Quilt Appraisal Certification Program, co-authored a number of books on quilts in the Pilgrim/Roy Collection, and served as interior designer for the Museum of the American Quilter's Society. Pilgrim and Roy also served as curators and designers for many MAQS exhibits, including the national "Gatherings: America's Quilt Heritage" project.

Many would agree with the friend and Pilgrim/Roy Interiors client who commented in response to Paul's death: "Paul was a life force. He gave us a beautiful legacy of art and love and humor. He was an endearing man and a wonderful friend."

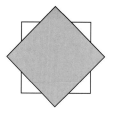

Introduction

Traditionally, quilt blocks and tops were pieced continuously to make practical use of spare time. Quilting, because it requires planning, space, and often additional help, was therefore arranged as need demanded. As a result, many more blocks and tops were made then quilts. It was not unusual for tops, blocks, and sewing materials to be saved and utilized by future generations. This accounts for many of the quilts we see today containing blocks and fabrics spanning many years.

In the early twentieth century when quiltmaking started to decline, many quilt related items were stored or thrown away. Completing or quilting inherited tops was customary in families where the craft continued from generation to generation without interruption. However, for those who came into quiltmaking later, this tradition was unfamiliar.

The idea of using old or antique blocks or tops seemed sacrilegious to contemporary quilters. The ongoing tradition of quiltmaking is rare today; therefore it is understandable why current attitudes of preserving, rather than using, prevail.

Paul Pilgrim's interest in antique tops, blocks, and fabrics for their historic and aesthetic value developed along with his interest in quilts. After completing a quilt from blocks left by his grandmother, he stretched the custom of using inherited pieces to include many unfinished projects from former unrelated generations. Ignoring criticism, convinced he was not only preserving by completion, but celebrating the efforts of anonymous quiltmakers from the past, he began incorporating antique blocks and fabrics into his own work.

Paul chose to incorporate not only ambitious efforts, but also simple, common, and sometimes primitive blocks. He had a remarkable ability to see the vitality in homely pieces that the rest of us might overlook. Many times I would question what he could possibly do with some of the odd pieces he bought. I was always amazed to see the results.

His knowledge of fabrics was extensive. He could tell by color, style, and method of printing when a fabric had been manufactured; however, he was not encumbered by this knowledge when designing quilts. When it came to choosing fabrics for his own work, he selected materials according to his own aesthetic needs. He had a remarkable ability to mentally catalog the patchwork pieces he collected. He would become very excited when he found pieces perfect for use with previous purchases — a number of years after the initial purchase. In the same quilt there might be fabrics or patchwork elements spanning over 75 years and purchased from different sources over of several years.

Paul's techniques have been widely imitated and his teaching has produced many finished quilts from countless unfinished projects. He has made a definite contribution in changing attitudes about preserving quiltmaking artifacts. His quilts and his teaching inadvertently rescued and preserved many wonderful examples of patchwork stored away in attics, basements, and barns.

Formally trained as an art teacher, his choice of medium for his own expression was collage. It is quite natural his work with fabric should take this direction. It is reassuring to know that the quilting tradition provides not only a broad opportunity for self expression, but also a built-in recycling system for unfinished projects. Especially those projects unappreciated during their time, but re-evaluated and reassured in another time by fresh and enthusiastic eyes.

We can all thank Paul for making us more aware.

One-Block Quilts
Celebrating a Single Design — and Often a Single Maker

The purpose for this quilt was to try and make a quilt that gave the feeling of a chintz quilt without using any chintz fabrics. The blocks in the quilt date from 1880 – 1890. It was a challenge to use a color scheme I had not used up to this point.

PAUL D. PILGRIM

Fabrics and Blocks

1 – Kaleidoscope block, 1910, Pennsylvania

2 – Centennial fabric designed by Jinny Beyer

3 – Contemporary print fabric, 1980

4 – Contemporary print, rose design, 1986

Kaleidoscope blocks are set on point

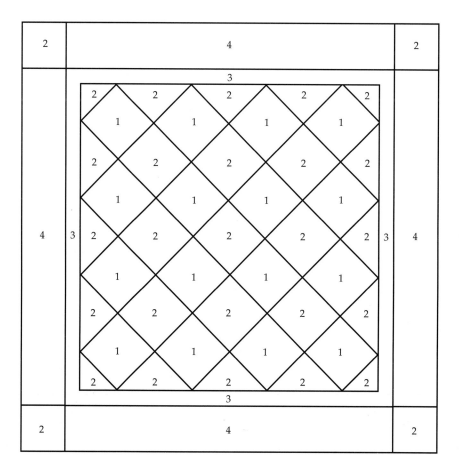

KALEIDOSCOPE

51" x 51", 1995

This is the first set of early wool Log Cabin blocks that I purchased from a dealer who had purchased the set of blocks from an Amish home in Lancaster, Pennsylvania. It is unusual to find sets of blocks or tops that were never finished. To find 60 such wonderful blocks made with these deep jewel tones was the find of a lifetime. I wanted to create something special with the blocks to make a contemporary quilt with its roots set in tradition. The wool blocks date from 1860.

PAUL D. PILGRIM

Fabrics and Blocks

1 – Log Cabin block, 1900, wool, Pennsylvania Mennonite

2 – Contemporary fabric

Binding and backing Contemporary fabrics

1		2								1
		2								
2	2	1	1	1	1	1	1	1	1	2	2
		1	1	1	1	1	1	1	1	
		1	1	1	1	1	1	1	1	
		1	1	1	1	1	1	1	1	
		1	1	1	1	1	1	1	1	
		1	1	1	1	1	1	1	1	
		1	1	1	1	1	1	1	1	
1		2								1
		2								

OFF-CENTER LOG CABIN

66" x 73", 1995

Log Cabin Straight Furrow blocks are set in an original design. This set of blocks was purchased in Pennsylvania years before Paul made this quilt. The border fabric was a new printed cotton but the corner blocks are of antique wool challis (c.1870) cut from yardage also purchased in Pennsylvania.

The corner block fabric was also the source of inspiration for the Alhambra Fabric Collection which Pilgrim/Roy designed for P&B Textiles in 1994.

Fabrics and Blocks

1 – Log Cabin block (wool), 1860 – 75, Pennsylvania

2 – Antique wool challis, purchased in Pennsylvania, c. 1870

3 – Contemporary fabric

Wool, wool challis, 1860 – 1875, Pennsylvania

2	3						2
	1	1	1	1	1	1	
	1	1	1	1	1	1	
3	1	1	1	1	1	1	3
	1	1	1	1	1	1	
	1	1	1	1	1	1	
2	3						2

LIGHTNING LOGS

60" x 54", 1990

This was a set of 16 blocks that I rescued from destruction. The blocks had been stored in an attic where mice had used part of the blocks to make a nest. When I found the blocks, they were in very bad condition. I took the blocks and replaced squares with antique fabric from the period and added the antique red fabric and completed the top using new fabric. The blocks date from 1860 – 1880.

PAUL D. PILGRIM

Fabrics and Blocks

1 – Nine-Patch block (with red fabrics), 1880, Pennsylvania

2 – Antique fabric, 1880, Pennsylvania

3 – Nine-Patch block (with green fabrics), 1880, Pennsylvania

4 – Antique fabric, 1880, Pennsylvania

5 – Antique fabric

6 – Contemporary fabric

Labyrinth pattern from the Pilgrim/Roy Alhambra line printed by P&B Textiles

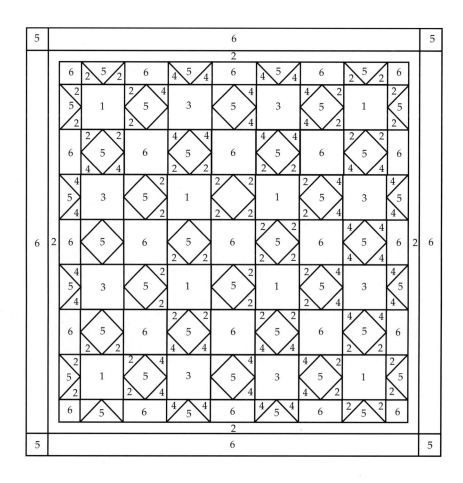

NINE-PATCH STARS

79" x 79", 1996

Each of these blocks, based on the Log Cabin technique, is from the 1875 – 1900 period. The red print on the border is new, as is the black print expanding the blocks.

This is one of the last tops of this type Paul completed. As he worked in this manner, he was satisfied to present simple and humble efforts rather than ambitious pieces of patchwork.

His taste in selecting blocks leaned toward those exhibiting spontaneous use of color and application — often those not so preoccupied with precision or accuracy. He felt there were plenty of other people who would collect the "fancy" ones. He searched for less obvious finds.

He would select blocks out of his "stash" that related to one another in terms of scale, color, and their makers' technical abilities. Sometimes there were not enough; so he devised this method of expanding what he had to fill the quilt and at the same time give each block the space it needed to be visually comfortable.

Fabrics and Blocks

1 – Log Cabin block or block segment, 1875 – 1900

2 – Contemporary fabrics

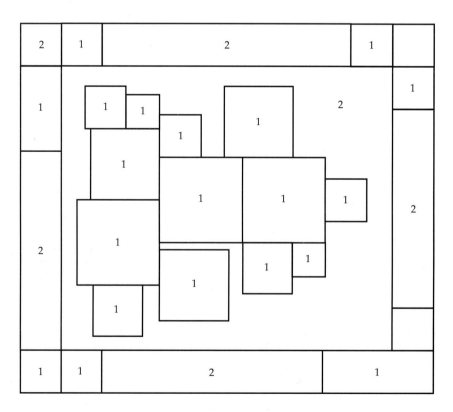

ASYMMETRICAL COMPOSITION

51" x 56½", 1992

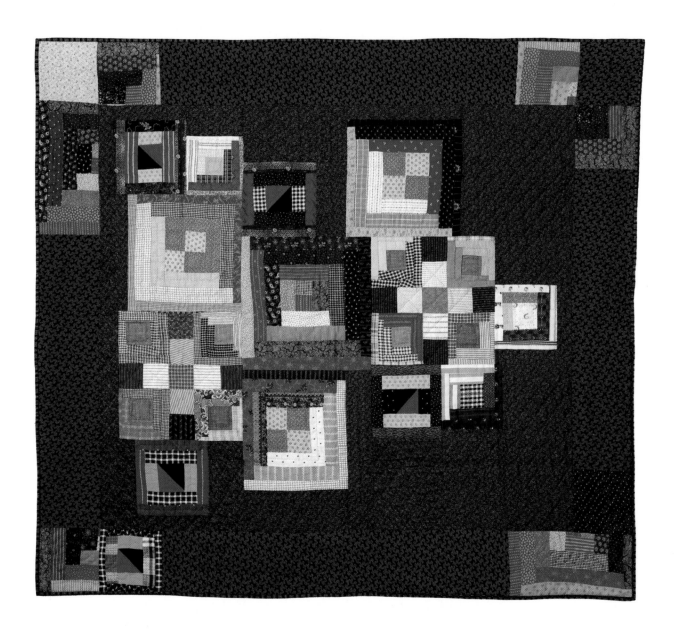

Two-Block Quilts
Pairing Patchwork Designs with Style

These blocks were purchased from Stella Rubin of Baltimore, Maryland. They are made of wonderful 1930s and 1940s fabrics. I made the trees from antique fabric as well as the lettering around the border. This is the first set of house blocks I had the pleasure of finding, and being able to purchase. This set of blocks caused great excitement when he found them. He agonized over purchasing them. They were more expensive than any set of blocks he had bought up to that time.

PAUL D. PILGRIM

Fabrics and Blocks

1 – House block, 1935, Maryland

2 – Tree block, made from 1890 fabrics, Pennsylvania

3 – Reproduction fabric (1930s), 1990, Marcus Brothers

4 – Reproduction fabric (1930s), 1990, Marcus Brothers

5 – Reproduction fabric, 1990

6 – Reproduction fabric, 1990, Marcus Brothers

7 – Antique fabrics, 1930, Pennsylvania

8 – Reproduction fabric

Binding and backing Contemporary fabrics

22

...HOME SWEET HOME...

79" x 79", 1994

When I received these nine large units of Bear's Paw blocks, they made me smile. There is no way I could take these blocks seriously. The quiltmaker had a great deal of trouble getting the pieces in the correct spot, which may be the reason the blocks were never completed. Lucky for me that the blocks were sent to me to enjoy. The blocks date from 1890 – 1900. I hope this quilt will leave you with a smile on your face and a new appreciation for funny blocks that need to be completed.

PAUL D. PILGRIM

Fabrics and Blocks

1 – Bear's Paw blocks, 1900,
    Pennsylvania

2 – Contemporary fabric, 1980,
    Marcus Brothers

3 – Contemporary fabric, 1985, India

4 – Antique fabric, 1900,
    Pennsylvania

5 – Log Cabin block, 1890,
    Pennsylvania

6 – Contemporary fabric, 1985

Binding and backing
Contemporary fabrics

BEAR'S PAW WITH PERSONALITY

78" x 78", 1995

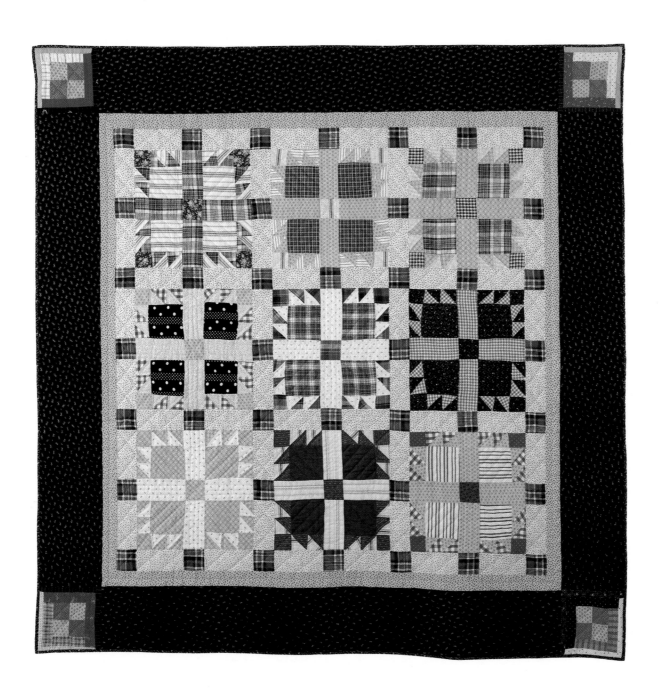

The blocks in this quilt are wonderful examples of fabric from 1860 – 1880. The fern border is a piece of fabric I found in Lancaster, Pennsylvania. The color quality in this quilt is very pleasing to me.

PAUL D. PILGRIM

Fabrics and Blocks

1 – Buckeye Beauty block, 1860 – 1880

2 – Nine-Patch block, 1880

3 – Antique fabrics, 1880

4 – Antique fabrics, 1890 – 1900

5 – Vintage fabric, 1950

Binding and backing
Contemporary fabric

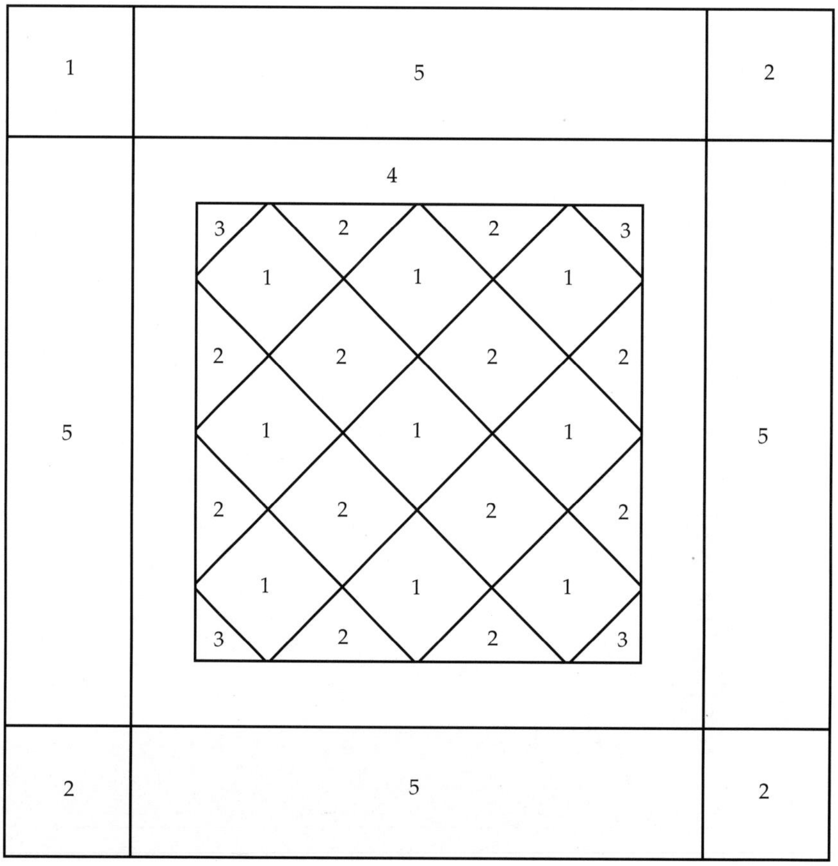

BUCKEYE BEAUTY

45" x 45", 1995

The blocks in this quilt all date from 1880 – 1885. They are deep saturated colors. It takes a while to see the Cactus Baskets in the design. I think that is why I enjoy the quilt so much.

PAUL D. PILGRIM

Fabrics and Blocks

1 – Birds in Air block, 1900

2 – Basket of Cherries, 1900

3 – Contemporary fabric

4 – Contemporary fabric

5 – Contemporary fabric (reproduction)

6 – Vintage fabric

Binding and backing
Contemporary fabrics

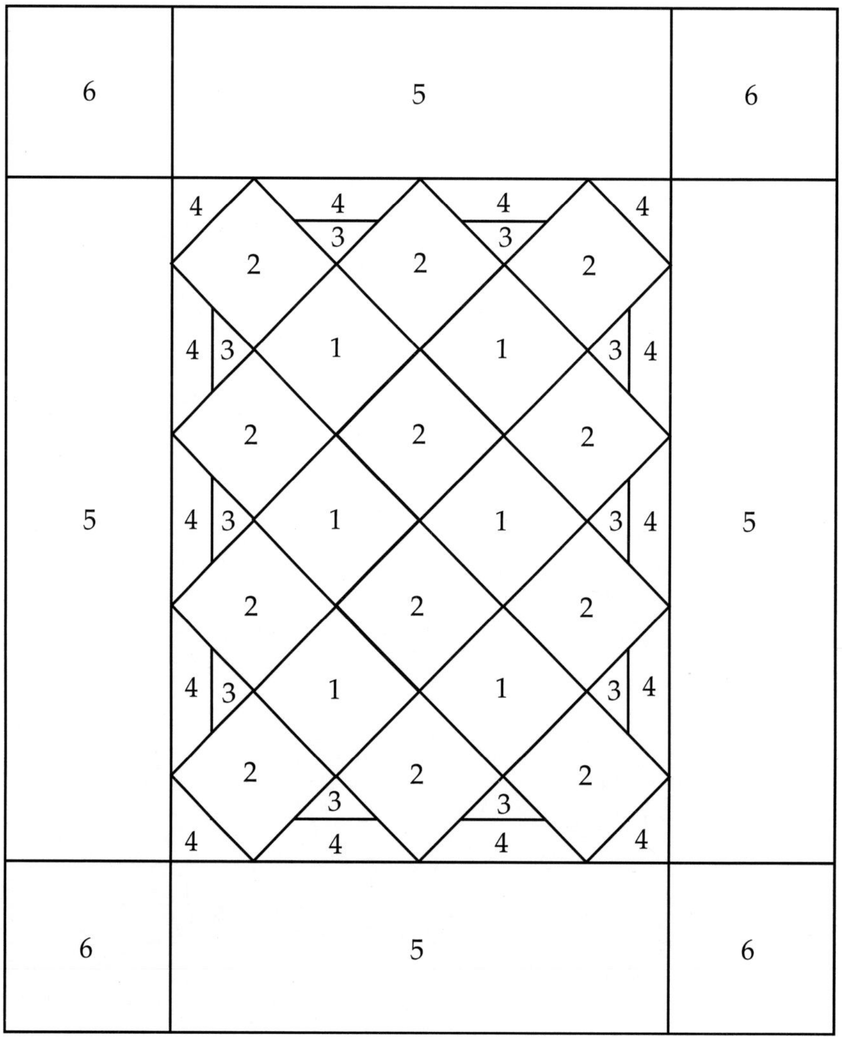

BIRDS AND BASKETS

57" x 64", 1995

The blocks in this top were all made in the 1930s. The blocks were so poorly made that I had to take the Bow Tie units apart to square them. I took the four sections apart one at a time so I could get the units together in the order the original quilt-maker had placed them. The Bow Tie triangle blocks around the edge of the quilt were made from antique fabrics to fill out the number of blocks necessary to complete my design. I also constructed these blocks in a different way so that in the future people will recognize that all these Bow Ties were not made by the same quiltmaker.

PAUL D. PILGRIM

Fabrics and Blocks

1 – Bow Tie block, 1940, Pennsylvania

1a – Bow Tie blocks with block segments, 1940, Pennsylvania

2 – Nine-Patch block, 1990 fabrics, P&B Textiles

2a – Nine-Patch block segment

3 – Contemporary plaid fabric, 1990, India

4 – Contemporary fabric, 1990, P&B Textiles

5 – Vintage fabric, 1940, Pennsylvania

6 – Contemporary fabric, 1990

7 – Contemporary plaid fabric, 1990

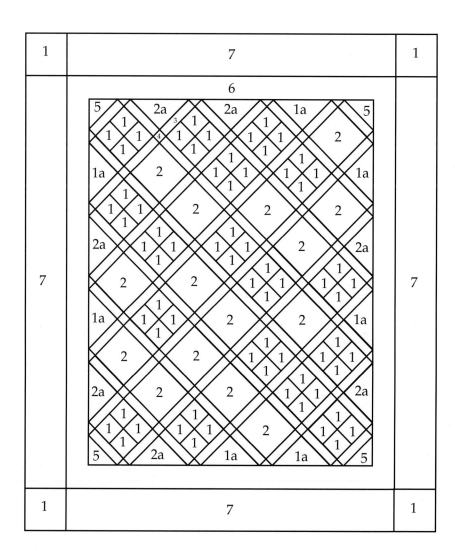

BOW TIES — EVERY COLOR, EVERY PATTERN
79" x 79", 1996

This quilt is one of my favorites. The blocks were made by the same person and purchased from Don (Donnie) Leiby, Humburg, Pennsylvania. For 20 years Donnie has been our greatest source of antique quilts, fabrics, and blocks. Without his help, we would never have been able to have the wonderful things we have in our collection or for me to use in my work.

I specifically like the color quality, simplicity, and elegance of these blocks. Because of their size I felt they needed to be presented in as large a quilt as possible; I devised this method to present them without interfering with them. The asymmetry seemed a natural way of blending the old blocks in a non-traditional composition.

PAUL D. PILGRIM

Fabrics and Blocks

1 – Double Four-Patch block, 1890, Pennsylvania

2 – Nine-Patch block, 1890, Pennsylvania

3 – Contemporary fabric

4 – Contemporary fabric

5 – Antique fabric, c.1890

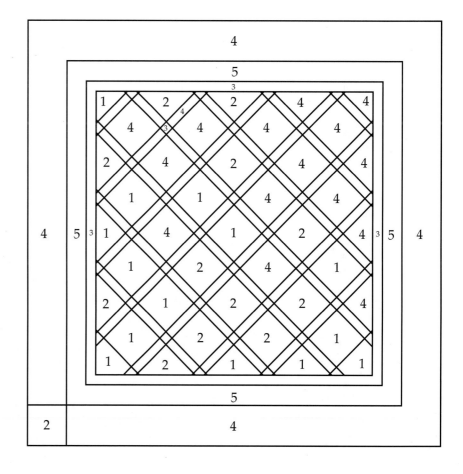

OLD BLOCKS EXPANDED

55½" x 55½", 1993

I am particularly taken with the simple elegance of the Double Four-Patch and Nine-Patch block forms. To make this arrangement successful, I had to select antique blocks that worked well together. After choosing 29 blocks, which I believe were all made by the same hand, I then set them in an asymmetrical arrangement, with counterpane blocks of my own that complemented and presented them and did not distract from their simple elegance.

These blocks were purchased in Lancaster, Pennsylvania. I am sure I have over the years purchased enough blocks to complete another dozen quilts. The blocks in this quilt date from 1880 – 1990.

PAUL D. PILGRIM

Fabrics and Blocks

1 – Double Four-Patch block, 1880 – 1890, Lancaster, Pennsylvania

2 – Nine-Patch block, newly constructed of antique fabrics, 1880 – 1890, Lancaster, Pennsylvania

3 – Contemporary fabrics

Binding and backing
Contemporary fabrics

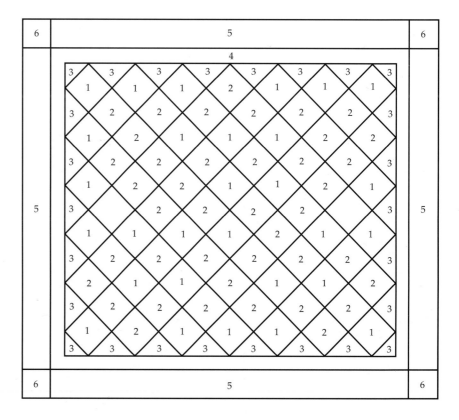

DOUBLE FOUR-PATCH ON POINT

70" x 62", 1996

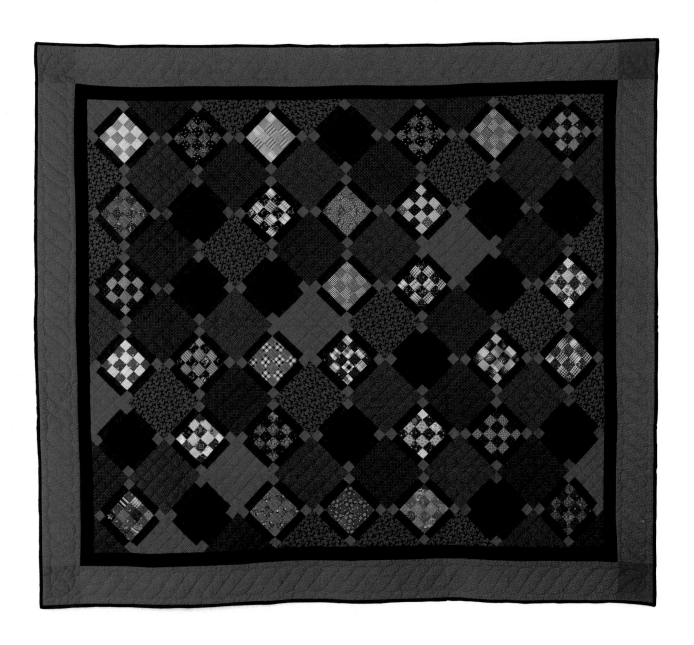

Combining Patchwork Strips, Sections & Blocks

Composing with a Multitude of Parts & Pieces

The blocks in this quilt were purchased from Kathy Sullivan and are from North Carolina. The color quality, size, and scale of the blocks worked well together to create a very pleasing overall pattern. For me, even the odd T's block with red was the perfect spark that finished off the quilt.

PAUL D. PILGRIM

Fabrics and Blocks

1 – Shoo Fly block, 1880, Pennsylvania

2 – Toad in a Puddle block, 1880, Pennsylvania

3 – Attic Window block, 1880, Pennsylvania

4 – T's block, 1880, Pennsylvania

5 – Antique fabric, 1890, Pennsylvania

6 – Contemporary fabric

7 – Antique fabrics, 1870 – 1890

Binding and backing
Contemporary fabrics

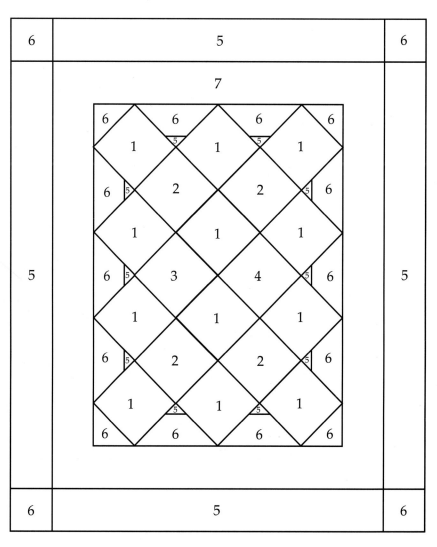

SHOO FLIES, TOADS & T'S

52" x 64", 1995

This set of 1940 round Dresden Plates, had never been appliquéd to a backing. They were purchased at Silver Dollar City Quilt Festival in Missouri from Helen Corlett, a quilt dealer. The 1940s Grandmother's Flower Garden blocks were part of a somewhat damaged top purchased in Springfield, Missouri, the same year.

These blocks were intentionally set against a dark blue fabric in contrast to their traditional set on muslin. This different set makes it very clear that these 1940s fabrics can be much more vibrant and active when set with a color rather than white.

This quilt was very different for me and fun to put together. These blocks — Dresden Plate and Grandmother's Flower Garden — were ones that I would never do myself.

PAUL D. PILGRIM

Fabrics and Blocks

1 – Dresden Plate block

1a– Quarter block

1b– Half block

2 – Grandmother's Flower Garden block

3 – Contemporary fabric

4 – Checkerboard made of contemporary fabric

Binding and backing Contemporary fabrics

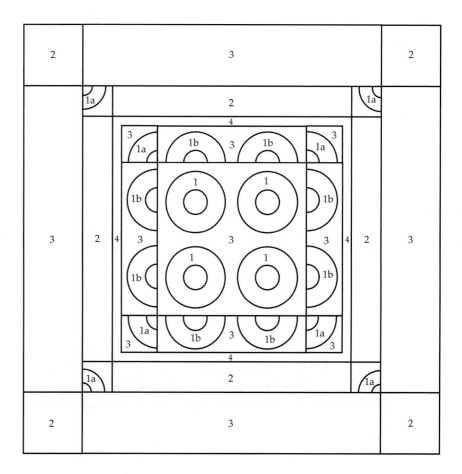

DRESDEN GARDEN

85" x 86", 1992

Paul bought a stack of blocks, 3½" squares made up of two pieces, one light and one dark, diagonally cut and sewn together. He arranged them into bars and set them with dark fabric to accentuate the "zigzag" created by the light triangles.

Some of the fabrics were so fragile that Paul was forced to interface each bar section after it had been sewn together, but before he joined the bars with the new fabric strips.

The antique Nine-Patch corner blocks on the outer border were also interfaced before they were placed in the quilt.

Fabrics and Blocks

1 – Bar of patchwork made of pieced
    3½" squares, 1870 – 1890

2 – Nine-Patch block, 1880

3 – Contemporary fabric

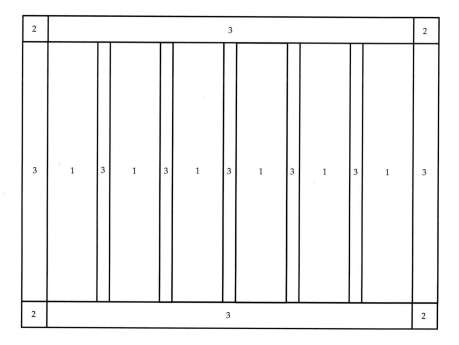

ZIGZAG BARS

66" x 52", c. 1989

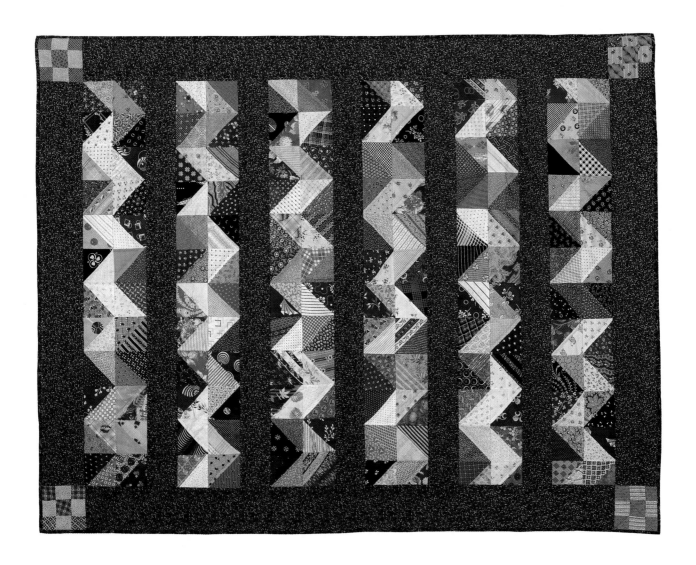

The strings of Geese in Flight patchwork were found as you see them, sewn together in strips, but never used. The Checkerboard patchwork sections were salvaged from a damaged top. The other blocks and fabrics were chosen for their restrained use of color. The intent was to allow the off-white elements in the design to be the focus of the quilt.

The blocks were cut diagonally, set on point, and sewn into bars in order to keep the construction consistent with the strings of Geese in Flight and the Checkerboard.

The red needs no explanation. When in doubt, use red!

The fragile nature of the early fabrics necessitated a certain amount of care and maintenance. This quilt would never survive were it to be used.

PAUL D. PILGRIM

Fabrics and Blocks

1 – Evening Star block, 1890, Pennsylvania

2 – Contemporary fabric

3 – Geese in Flight patchwork, 1875 (some earlier fabrics included), Pennsylvania

4 – Antique Victorian print, 1880, Pennsylvania

5 – Checkerboard Patchwork (salvaged sections of an old top), 1840, Pennsylvania

6 – Peek-a-Boo block (divided in half by Geese), 1890, Pennsylvania

7 – Old Maid's Puzzle block segment (Madder print fabrics), 1865, Pennsylvania

8 – Double Cross block segment, 1880, Pennsylvania

9 – Old Maid's Puzzle block segment, 1880

10 – Churn Dash block (half a block), 1880, Pennsylvania

Binding and backing Contemporary fabrics

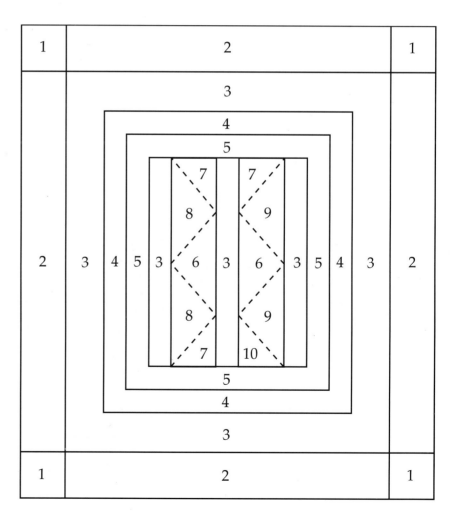

GEESE ALL AROUND

51" x 55", 1989

The Inner border allowed the use of the Geese in Flight strips remaining from "Geese All Around."

These wonderful little 1870 Nine-Patch blocks are from Pennsylvania and are all that existed. Their scale dictated the size of the quilt and their color proved to be very compatible with the remaining strips of geese. The outer border is 1880 fabric.

Corner blocks are 1875 LeMoyne Star blocks made in madder prints. The plaid corner blocks in the geese border are new.

Fabrics and Blocks

1 – Geese in Flight patchwork strips, 1875 (some earlier fabrics), Pennsylvania

2 – Nine-Patch block, 1870, Pennsylvania

3 – LeMoyne Star block, 1875 (madder prints)

4 – Vintage fabric, 1950

3	4					3
	4	1			4	
4	1	2 2 2 2 2			1	4
		2 2 2 2 2				
		2 2 2 2 2				
		2 2 2 2 2				
		2 2 2 2 2				
		2 2 2 2 2				
	4	1			4	
3	4					3

GEESE AROUND NINE

38" x 42", 1991

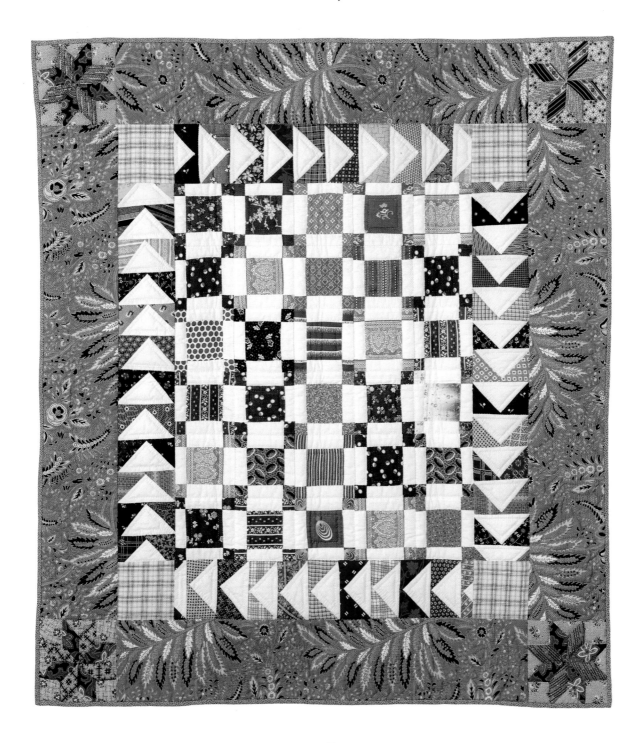

On a trip to Hamburg, Pennsylvania, my friend, Don Leiby, offered me a strip of Carolina Lily blocks that had been cut in half and sewn together with some single patches. I took the single patch strips off the lilies and began designing the center strip and the two outside strips. I wonder why a quiltmaker would cut her beautiful blocks in such a manner. I like to think the blocks were inherited by a second wife and she was tired of hearing what a wonderful quiltmaker the first wife had been. These blocks date from 1870 – 1890.

PAUL D. PILGRIM

Fabrics and Blocks

1 – Many Pointed Star block segment, 1890, Pennsylvania

2 – Irish Chain or Double Nine-Patch block segments, 1890

3 – Bricks block, 1890, Pennsylvania

4 – One Patch block, 1890, Pennsylvania

5 – Lilies block (segment cut from a row of blocks), 1875, Pennsylvania

6 – Square in a Square block framed with Star of the Milky Way block segments, 1890, Pennsylvania

7 – LeMoyne Star, 1890, Pennsylvania

8 – Contemporary fabric

Binding and backing
Contemporary fabrics

WHO CUT THE LILIES

84" x 76", 1996

This quilt was made to display at Christmas. I chose bold patterns and a simple composition so that the quilt could hold its own with other holiday decorations.

The blocks were chosen because they reminded me of Christmas. When I set about to make the quilt, I was pressured in that the window of our antique store needed to be dressed for Christmas — and soon.

In going through my blocks, I had a very limited number that would be appropriate, in fact, only these. I set them this way because it was the only way to handle so few blocks.

I remember a quilt collector coming into the store to purchase the piece, which was only a top at the time. She couldn't believe it was new, made of old blocks, and was furious because I wouldn't sell it to her.

PAUL D. PILGRIM

Fabrics and Blocks

1 – Peony block, c. 1890,
    Pennsylvania

2 – Cactus block segment, c. 1890,
    Pennsylvania

3 – Basket block, c. 1890,
    Pennsylvania

4 – Fleur-de-lis block, c. 1860,
    Pennsylvania

5 – Antique fabric, c. 1880

6 – Antique fabric, 1880

7 – Contemporary fabric

    Binding and backing
    Contemporary fabric

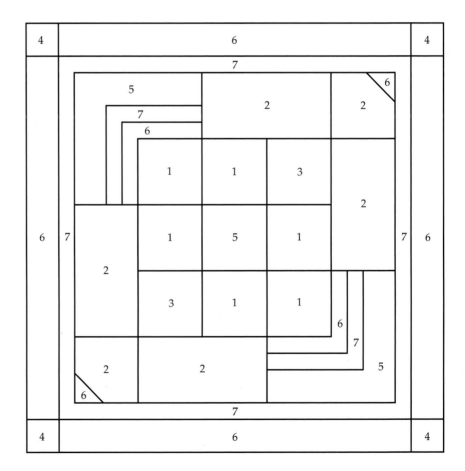

CHRISTMAS QUILT
55¾" x 55", 1990

At first it looks random. Notice how Paul places the Log Cabin blocks to create the panel of light going from upper left to lower right diagonally through the quilt.

It is a combination of blocks which are all from the same period: 1870 – 1890. Only two block designs are used for the interior: Divided Cross and Four-Patch Log Cabin. The sashing and corner blocks are made of new fabric. The inner frame is a Pilgrim/Roy Seaweed design from P&B Textiles. The outer border is also new fabric.

The Star of the East corner blocks in the outer border are antique.

The large border of antique blocks outside the sashed blocks is made of antique Log Cabin blocks with a diagonal center rather than square. The four corner blocks in this border are "crazy."

This is one of the quilts I found after Paul's death; the information, name, and date are from me.

Fabrics and Blocks

1 – Divided Cross block, 1870 – 1890, Pennsylvania

2 – Four-Patch Log Cabin block, 1870 – 1890, Pennsylvania

3 – Crazy patch block

4 – Log Cabin blocks with diagonal centers, 1870 – 1890, Pennsylvania

5 – Star of the East block, 1870 – 1890, Pennsylvania

6 – Contemporary fabric, "Seaweed" from the Pilgrim/Roy Collection (P&B Textiles)

7 – Contemporary fabrics

Binding and backing Contemporary fabrics

50

PENNSYLVANIA DUTCH BLOCKS

84" x 84", c. 1993

Sampler Quilts
Integrating a Glorious Profusion of Blocks

This quilt was designed and constructed to illustrate how to set old blocks with a variety of techniques. The blocks were selected for their ability to work together in a traditional sampler style quilt where all the blocks are the same size and set within a grid and then bordered.

Old and new fabrics as well as parts of old tops and blocks have been used to accomplish this.

Fabrics and Blocks

All blocks c. 1875 – 1900

1 – Unnamed or Arrowhead Puzzle Variation block, contemporary fabrics used to extend the block

2 – Pinwheel block, antique fabric used to extend block

3 – Variable Star block, contemporary fabrics used to extend the block on two sides

4 – Jacob's Ladder block, antique fabrics used to extend block

5 – Ducks and Ducklings block, antique fabrics used to extend block

6 – Basket block, antique fabric used to extend

7 – Churn Dash block, remnants of antique top used to extend the block on two sides

8 – Odd Fellows block, antique fabric used to extend block

9 – Variable Star block, antique tops and blocks, along with two pieces of contemporary royal blue fabric, used to extend block

10 – Double X block, antique fabrics used to extend block

11 – House block

12 – Variable Star block, antique fabric used to extend block

13 – Basket block, antique fabrics, 1890–1900, contemporary fabrics used to extend the block

14 – Blocks in a Box Variation block, antique fabrics also used to extend block

15 – English Dog block, antique fabrics used to extend block

16 – Ducks & Ducklings block, antique fabrics used to extend block

17 – Log Cabin block, antique fabrics

18 – Churn Dash block, new fabrics used to extend block

19 – Variable Star, Antique Log Cabin top used to extend block

20 – Double Z block, antique fabrics

21 – Contemporary fabric

22 – Antique fabric

23 – Contemporary fabric

Binding antique; same as sashing

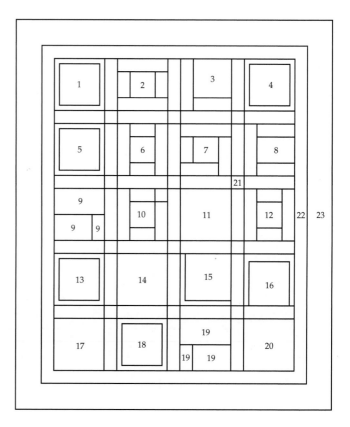

SASHED SAMPLER

44" x 65", 1990

This quilt contains antique Indigo blue and Cadet blue blocks collected from Pennsylvania to California. Blocks date from 1880 to 1900. The four 1880 Star blocks and three 1880 Churn Dash blocks are believed to have been made by the same maker. All other blocks were "orphan blocks." Some were used in their entirety. Others were cut to fill in where necessary. I squeezed every thread out of those remnants! There wasn't even enough left for floss.

PAUL D. PILGRIM

Fabrics and Blocks

1 – Evening Star block, 1890

2 – Churn Dash block, 1890

2a – Churn Dash block segment cut by Paul to fit space, 1890

3 – Jacob's Ladder block segment, 1890

4 – Goose in the Pond block (parts of a whole), 1880

5 – Four-Patch block, 1900

5a – Four-Patch block segment

6 – Aunt Sukey's Choice block, 1890

7 – Basket block, 1890, extended with segments of antique blocks

8 – Log Cabin block, 1900

9 – Maple Leaf block, 1890

10 – Album block, 1890

11 – The Jig Saw Puzzle, 1880

12 – Evening Star, 1900

13 – Contemporary fabrics

14 – Log Cabin block segment

Binding and backing
Contemporary fabrics

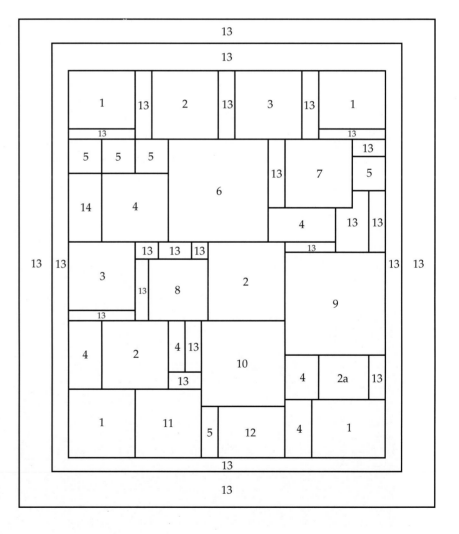

BITS & PIECES SAMPLER

48" x 55", 1993

The appliqué blocks in this quilt were collected over a period of five years. The majority of the blocks were purchased from quilt dealers in Pennsylvania, Vermont, and Kentucky. All the blocks date from 1860 – 1880.

PAUL D. PILGRIM

The large center appliqué block was already faded when Paul placed it in the composition. It had been faded when he purchased it.

Fabrics and Blocks

1 – Fleur-de-lis block or portion of fleur-de-lis block, 1860, Pennsylvania
   1a – entire block
   1b – ½ block
   1c – ¼ block

2 – Old Fashioned Rose block, 1870, Pennsylvania

3 – Centennial Wreath block, 1870, Pennsylvania, found basted to muslin. Elise B. Roy (Jerry's mother) appliquéd it for me to be able to use it in this quilt.

4 – Foundation Rose Wreath block, 1880, Pennsylvania

5 – Tulip block, 1870, Pennsylvania

6 – Oak Leaf and Reel block, 1870, Pennsylvania

7 – Variable Star block, 1870, Pennsylvania

8 – Tulips block, 1860, Pennsylvania

9 – Honey Bee block, 1870, Pennsylvania

10 – Laurel Leaves block, 1870, Pennsylvania

11 – Reverse Appliqué Fan block, 1880, Pennsylvania

12 – Four Lilies block, 1870, Pennsylvania

13 – "Cloth of Gold" vintage fabric, 1940

14 – Antique fabric, 1900, Pennsylvania

15 – Antique fabrics, extented sashings, c. 1900

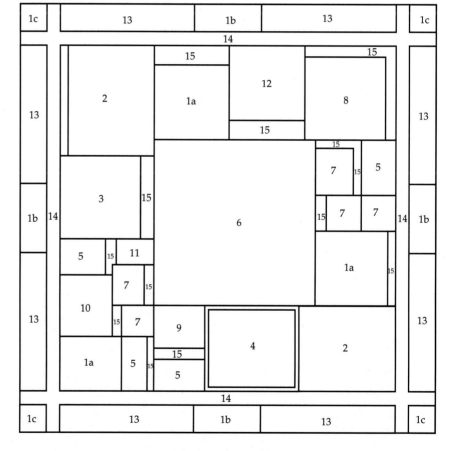

ANTIQUE SAMPLER

77" x 77", 1993

The blocks used in this quilt were purchased in Pennsylvania and Kentucky, at two locations. Often it takes me a long time to get the blocks together before I start one of my quilts. These blocks were collected over a very short period of time, and I began working on the quilt as soon as I had enough blocks to create the design you see here. Blocks date from 1900 – 1920.

PAUL D. PILGRIM

Fabrics and Blocks

1 – Baseball block, 1930s, Kentucky

2 – Ocean Waves block, 1910, Pennsylvania

3 – Nine-Patch block segment, 1930, Pennsylvania

4 – Red & white check fabric, 1910, Pennsylvania

5 – Vintage print fabric, 1930, Pennsylvania

6 – Contemporary fabric

Binding and backing
New fabric

SAMPLER B

62" x 62", 1992

This quilt was made from nineteenth century blocks and pieces from a damaged Log Cabin top. The center of the quilt also uses fragments of old blocks to complete the design. The sampler is also a center medallion. Borders radiating from the four center blocks on point are composed of bits and pieces of tops and blocks. The design is then squared by using remnants of a damaged Log Cabin top.

PAUL D. PILGRIM

Fabrics and Blocks

1 – Log Cabin block or block segment, 1880, Pennsylvania

2 – Jacob's Ladder block, 1890, Pennsylvania

3 – Variable Star block, 1890, Pennsylvania

4 – Monkey Wrench block, 1900, Pennsylvania

5 – Nine-Patch block, 1900, Pennsylvania

6 – Basket block, 1900, Pennsylvania

7 – Log Cabin block, 1890, Pennsylvania

8 – Dove at the Window block, 1900, Pennsylvania

9 – Duck and Ducklings block segment, 1900, Pennsylvania

10 – Bachelor's Puzzle block, 1890, Pennsylvania

11 – Double X block, 1890, Pennsylvania

12 – Eight Point Star block, 1890, Pennsylvania

13 – One-Patch block, 1900, Pennsylvania

14 – Miscellaneous block fragments, 1900, Pennsylvania

15 – Four-Patch, 1900, Pennsylvania

16 – Contemporary fabric

17 – Contemporary new fabric

Border, binding, and backing New fabric

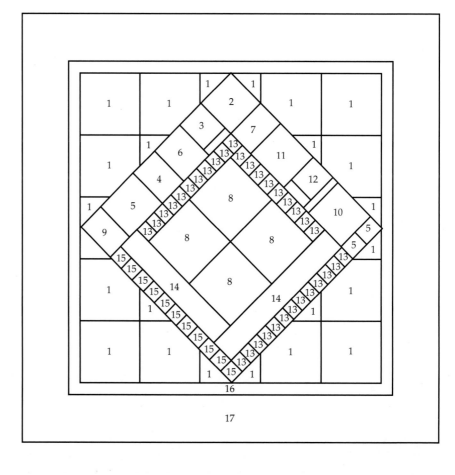

SAMPLER A
73" x 73", 1989

This quilt was made from blocks found on several trips through Pennsylvania. The majority of the blocks were found in and around Lancaster, Pennsylvania. I have always been attracted to the strong color found in Pennsylvania Dutch quilts, and I have been able to gather enough blocks to make several of these bold-colored quilts. The blocks in this quilt all date from 1875 – 1890.

PAUL D. PILGRIM

Fabrics and Blocks

1 – Sunburst block, 1880, Pennsylvania

2 – Double T's block, 1900, Pennsylvania

3 – LeMoyne Star block, 1890, Pennsylvania

4 – Beggar's block, 1880, Pennsylvania

5 – Basket block, 1875, Pennsylvania

6 – Crossroads to Texas block, 1875, Pennsylvania

7 – Wedding Ring block, 1875, Pennsylvania

8 – LeMoyne Star block, 1890, Pennsylvania

9 – Log Cabin block, 1880, Pennsylvania

10 – Antique fabric, 1885

11 – Log Cabin block segments, 1880, Pennsylvania

12 – Sixteen-Patch block segments, 1880, Pennsylvania

13 – Vintage fabric, 1900

14 – Vintage fabric, 1900

15 – Four-Patch block, 1900, Pennsylvania

Binding and backing
Contemporary fabrics

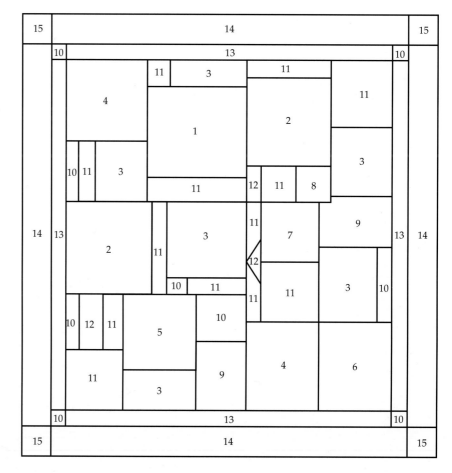

DUTCH SAMPLER

62" x 62", 1996

This quilt is made up of mostly 1930s quilt blocks. There are three Ocean Wave blocks from 1890. The challenge for me was to get these oversized blocks to fit into this quilt. This was a real challenge for me since I do not use such large scale blocks in my work. I now have enough 30s blocks to attempt another quilt in similar fabrics, but smaller scale.

PAUL D. PILGRIM

Fabrics and Blocks

1 – Young Man's Fancy block, 1930s, Pennsylvania

2 – Oceans Waves block, 1910, Pennsylvania

3 – Nine-Patch block, 1930s, Pennsylvania

4 – Checkerboard block, 1930s, Pennsylvania

5 – Snail's Trail block, 1930, Pennsylvania

6 – Vintage fabric, 1940, Pennsylvania

7 – Cotton Reel

8 – Contemporary

Binding and backing
Contemporary fabrics

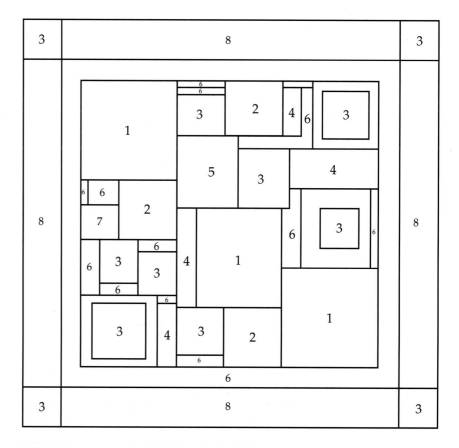

1930s SAMPLER
74" x 74", 1992

"Sew Them As They Are" is constructed using the crooked seam lines determined by the shape of the block as it was found. Rather than trimming or trying to disguise the crooked blocks, he used the same contrasting sashing fabric to fill in the uneven spaces between the sashing and the blocks.

Fabrics and Blocks

1 – Double X block, 1875, Pennsylvania

2 – Ohio Star block, 1880 – 1885, Pennsylvania

3 – Log Cabin patchwork segments, 1900

4 – Geese in Flight patchwork segments, 1900, Pennsylvania

5 – Grape Basket block, 1890, Pennsylvania

6 – School House block, 1875, Kentucky, from Helen Thompson

7 – Tea Leaf block, 1900, Pennsylvania

8 – Snail's Trail block/Indiana Puzzle, 1890, Allentown, Pennsylvania

9 – Double T's, 1900, Kentucky

10 – Mosaic, 1900, Missouri

11 – Patchwork fragments, 1890 – 1900

12 – Ohio Star block, 1900, North Carolina, from Kathy Sullivan

13 – North Carolina Lily block, 1870

14 – Furnishing fabrics, 1875 – 1880, Pennsylvania

15 – Unique Basket block, 1890 – 1900

16 – Corn and Beans block, 1870, Pennsylvania

17 – Evening Star block, 1875, Pennsylvania

18 – Rocky Road segment, 1900, Pennsylvania

19 – Pinwheel block, 1900, Pennsylvania

20 – Fabric Square, 1870

21 – Fabric Square, 1875

22 – Geese in Flight patchwork segment, 1890

23 – Geese in Flight patchwork segment, 1890

24 – Churn Dash block, 1875, Pennsylvania

25 – Contemporary fabric

26 – Nine-Patch on Point, 1875, Pennsylvania

27 – Antique green fabric, 1880, used as sashing around blocks and in corner blocks

Backing and binding
Contemporary fabrics

*Note — All blocks appear in the quilt with sashing around them, pieced from antique green fabric #27. Sashing is not indicated as separate from the block on the diagram.

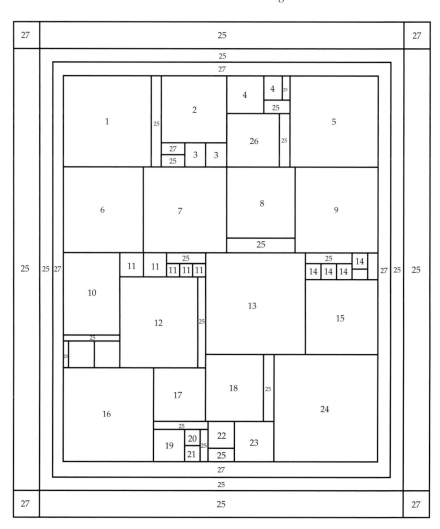

SEW THEM AS THEY ARE

70¾" x 62½", 1994

This quilt relates to Paul's other expanded block technique. It is the only example of a sampler using the same method. Even with the sampler form it became less important to fill the entire surface with patchwork. Paul's style, in his later work, takes on a simplicity and pure manner allowing each block to stand alone and yet remain part of the whole design.

I remember him spending hours pouring over his collection of blocks, selecting the ones to use in a specific quilt. He would often say, "Look at this — wouldn't you love to meet this person?

Fabrics and Blocks

1 – Variable Star block, 1870 – 1890

2 – Beggar's Block Variation, 1870 – 1890, Pennsylvania

3 – Jacob's Ladder block, 1870 – 1890, Pennsylvania

4 – Nine-Patch Straight Furrow block, 1870 – 1890, Pennsylvania

5 – Expanded Season block, 1870 – 1890, Pennsylvania

6 – Divided Cross block, 1870 – 1890, Pennsylvania

7 – Texas Star block, 1870 – 1890, Pennsylvania

8 – Basket block, 1870 – 1890, Pennsylvania

9 – Variable Star block, 1870 – 1890, Pennsylvania

10 – Grandmother's Pride block, 1860, Pennsylvania

11 – Lone Star block, 1870 – 1890, Pennsylvania

12 – Duck's Foot block, 1870 – 1890, Pennsylvania

13 – Right and Left block, 1870 – 1890, Pennsylvania

14 – Gentlemen's Fancy block, 1870 – 1890, Pennsylvania

15 – Antique fabric

16 – Contemporary fabric

17 – Contemporary fabric

18 – Contemporary fabric

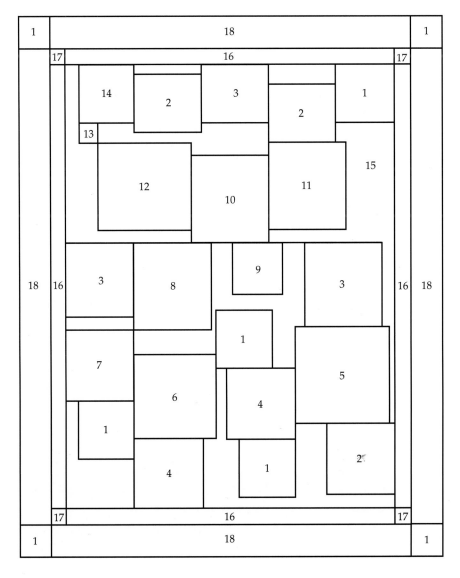

68

EXPANDED SAMPLER

56" x 72", 1995

Tips for Blending the Old & the New

Old patchwork blocks and pieces are often very inspiring — and using them in new quilts can promote great resourcefulness and creativity. Paul's quilts and his comments about their development provide wonderful ideas for design and technique.

To plan a quilt, Paul would first choose the blocks he wanted to use. Sometimes that would happen quickly. Often, however, he would construct the blocks over an extended period of time. There was great variety in the types of blocks he integrated in a quilt and the way he went about composing it.

Sometimes he picked blocks relating to a particular theme as for the "Christmas Quilt," page 49. Other blocks Paul related by date or region, as in "Birds and Baskets," page 29. In some he combined different blocks made by the same person.

Once he had assembled the patchwork elements, Paul selected fabrics for completing the quilt. He generally used new fabrics for the backing and binding and elsewhere, if appropriate. Frequently he used vintage fabrics as well.

Then he drafted a scale drawing of the quilt, like the one for "Sew Them As They Are," shown at right. He positioned the old blocks that had inspired the quilt and then graphed them into the diagram. He planned what elements he could use to fill the remaining open spaces. It was not unusual for him to determine the finished quilt size to a large extent by the size, number, and shape of the antique blocks that were available.

If there were not enough old blocks for what he wanted to do, Paul would construct new blocks to complement the antique ones. Other times he would select a second set of antique blocks to include. He used Nine-Patch with Buckeye Beauty (p. 27), Cactus Baskets with Birds & Baskets (p. 29), and many other fascinating combinations. He always planned these pairings carefully, so that the blocks at the heart of the quilt were shown to their best advantage and not overpowered.

Paul prepared the blocks next, carefully pressing them and solving any problems such as straightening the edges. Occasionally he had to take the blocks apart completely and

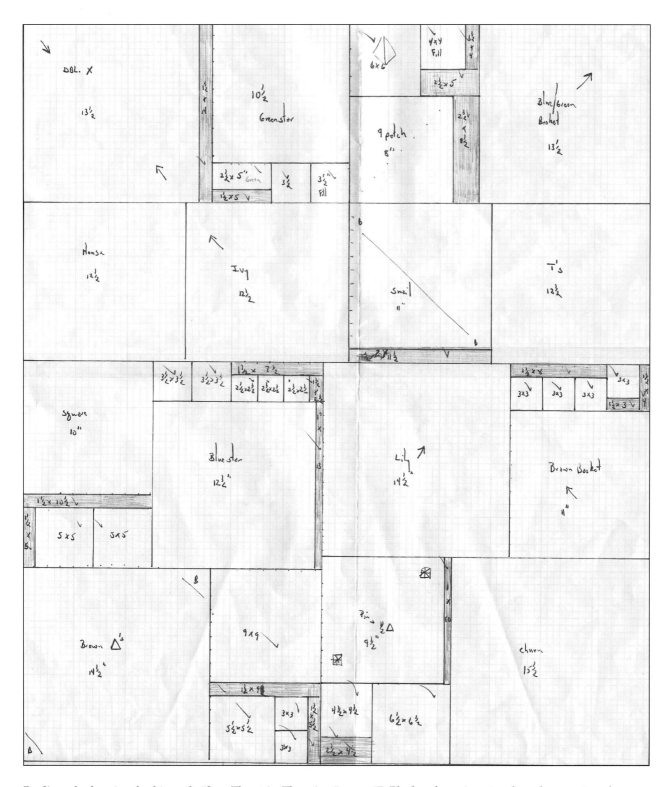

Paul's scale drawing for his quilt "Sew Them As They Are," page 67. Blocks of varying sizes have been assigned spaces and drawn to scale, with measurements noted. Filler squares and stripes have been added. Note the arrows indicating the direction the image or images in a block will fall. Borders are not included in the diagram.

reassemble them. Or he might trim them to eliminate stains, damaged areas, or holes, or to square a block. Paul also learned that if a block had no seam allowance, he could still use the center portions. He also made blocks larger by adding borders on one or more sides.

Frequently appliqué blocks are found just basted to the background or partially finished. If the background area was stained, Paul might replace it before stitching the shapes in place. He always tried to substitute period rather than new muslin. When the blocks were ready to use, he constructed the quilt according to plan, making adjustments as necessary.

Paul prepared the blocks next, carefully pressing them and solving any problems he discovered, making them more regular of the correct size for use. There were times when blocks were taken entirely apart and resewn. Sometimes the solution would be trimming to eliminate stains, damaged areas, or holes, or to make a block square or the right size. Paul also discovered that when a block had no seam allowance, he could still use center portions, creating a smaller block with the needed allowance. Blocks could also be made larger, through the addition of borders on one or more sides.

Above: Patchwork bits and pieces collected by Paul for use in his quilts. The bold 1890s LeMoyne Star block and half block on top of the patchwork remnants are undoubtedly left over from his construction of his "Dutch Sampler" quilt on page 63 and several other quilts. He saved even the half and quarter sections of antique blocks for possible future use. The full LeMoyne Star block offers insights into the missing points in his "Dutch Sampler" quilts — the antique blocks included no seam allowance.

Following are some ideas and tips that might be of help to you if you are about to recycle some "orphan blocks" from the past.

How can sets of blocks be used?

• By themselves, set solid

• By themselves, set with lattice or sashing

• In combination with strips of patchwork

• With elements added to create a new block

• In combination with a second antique block

• In combination with a second block created specially for the quilt

Above: Detail showing four Bear's Paw blocks that are joined with sashing and corner squares. "Bear's Paw with Personality," page 25.

Left: Detail showing five antique Cactus Basket blocks combined with three Birds in Air blocks from the same period. Note the Cactus Basket blocks all face in one direction, but the direction of the Birds in Air blocks varies. In the overall quilt the placement of these blocks is balanced. "Birds and Baskets," page 29.

How can you use an odd block or two?

• As corner squares for inner or outer borders in a quilt made from another pattern

• As a centerpiece of the design, whole or split with other patchwork between the parts

• Cut into half or quarter blocks which can be positioned symmetrically in the quilt design

Page 74

Top: Detail showing the use of an 1880 Nine-Patch block as a corner square in a quilt composed of 1870 – 1890 Bar patchwork. "Zigzag Bars," page 41. Paul sometimes used matching blocks in corners, and other times used different designs in some corners.

Bottom: Detail showing a graphic quilt center composed of various blocks and block segments. Note the combination of half and quarter Cactus Blocks framing a center created from six Peony and two Basket blocks. Used in this fashion, patchwork blocks can be engineered to beautifully fill whatever space is available. "Christmas Quilt," page 49.

Page 75

Top: Center quilt detail showing a strip of 1875 Geese in Flight patchwork dividing in half a Peek-a-Boo block in the center, and positioned between two segments of two Double Cross Blocks on the strip's left and two Old Maid's block segments on the strip's right. Other Old Maid's block segments and a Churn Dash segment complete the quilt center. "Geese All Around," page 43.

Below: Center quilt detail showing a Many Pointed Star block cut in half and positioned on either side of a patchwork strip. "Who Cut the Lilies," page 47.

How can you fill an open space in a quilt design?

• Make a new block from antique fabrics of the same period

• Cut a section from an antique block

• Cut a section from a patchwork piece composed of several blocks. Quilt tops that are severely damaged often have areas that can be used intact in this way. Paul never cut up quilts that had been completed, only unquilted tops and blocks.

• Cut one piece that shape from antique yardage

• Cut one piece from contemporary fabric that integrates well with the antique blocks

• Cut one piece from contemporary reproduction fabric

Above and Below: Details showing the way various antique blocks and patchwork segments are used to fill empty space in Paul's quilt "Sew Them As They Are," diagramed on page 71 and shown in full color on page 67. Note the complex combinations of blocks and pieces and the way that even a fraction of a block integrates well and adds interest to the quilt.

Above: Detail showing how Tree blocks made using 1890 fabrics and sashing pieces cut from reproduction fabrics were used to fill in spaces for a quilt inspired by 1930s House blocks. "...Home Sweet Home...," page 23.

How can you make a block the right size for your quilt?

• Seam it in to fit, even if that involves cutting off points. This can work well in some quilt designs.

• Take the block apart and re-sew the seams. This can be helpful if the problem is the result of imperfect construction.

• Add borders cut from antique or contemporary fabric as needed. These borders can be added to all sides or fewer.

• Add borders cut from a patchwork block of a different design.

Top: Corner from "Dutch Sampler" showing LeMoyne Star blocks seamed in to fit, with corners cut off. These bold blocks add much to the quilt, and are integrated so cleverly that one tends not to notice their missing points. "Dutch Sampler," page 63. Note also the patchwork bits and pieces seamed in to fit whatever space remained open.

Bottom: Top section of "Bits & Pieces Sampler," with its many examples of ways to make a block fit. Fabric strips and patchwork bits and pieces combine to make blocks of various sizes integrate well in this quilt. "Bits & Pieces Sampler," page 55.

As you work with old pieces in new quilts, you'll discover your own ways of making certain you can include those bits and pieces of the past that have inspired you. As you work, remember to have a good deal of fun as you create. Paul always did!

Above: These blocks are several from a full set of antique string-pieced star blocks Paul had carefully pressed in preparation for his next quilt blending the old and the new. We can imagine great fun Paul would have had celebrating these bright patchwork pieces.

AQS Books on Quilts

This is only a partial listing of the books on quilts that are available from the American Quilter's Society. AQS books are known the world over for their timely topics, clear writing, beautiful color photographs, and accurate illustrations and patterns. Most of the following books are available from your local bookseller, quilt shop, or public library. If you are unable to locate certain titles in your area, you may order by mail from the AMERICAN QUILTER'S SOCIETY, P.O. Box 3290, Paducah, KY 42002-3290. Customers with Visa or MasterCard may phone in orders from 7:00–5:00 CST, Monday–Friday, Toll Free 1-800-626-5420. Add $2.00 for postage for the first book ordered and $0.40 for each additional book. Include item number, title, and price when ordering. Allow 14 to 21 days for delivery.